THEN & NOW

AROUND GERMANTOWN

OPPOSITE: A Germantown landmark for close to a century, the Cider Barrel tells its own story in this image: "We Bow Before the Volstead Act and Serve It to You Sweet. Tis Better Far Than Old and Hard This Glorious Temperance Treat." The last glass of cider was served in 2002. (Courtesy of Jean King Phillips and Irving Abb.)

THEN & NOW

AROUND GERMANTOWN

Margaret Coleman

To Drew Edyth, born January 22, 2008

ISBN 978-0-7385-5416-7

Library of Congress control number: 2008922143

Published by Arcadia Publishing
Charleston, South Carolina

Printed in the United States of America

For all general information contact Arcadia Publishing at:
Telephone 843-853-2070
Fax 843-853-0044
E-mail sales@arcadiapublishing.com
For customer service and orders:
Toll-Free 1-888-313-2665

Visit us on the Internet at www.arcadiapublishing.com

On the Front Cover: E. Francis Baldwin designed this small railroad station for Germantown. Built in 1891, the building burned in 1979. With the advent of Germantown growth, a new station was built following the old design. Today the busy rail stop and adjoining parking lot blend history with fast, reliable mass transportation. Even the county council chairman takes the train from Germantown. (Both, author's collection.)

On the Back Cover: Germantown, Maryland, is a new city. Until 1980, it was a quiet, rural community of farms and cows with a few new houses built for employees of the Atomic Energy Commission. When Maryland-National Capital Park and Planning Commission adopted the area, everything changed. No cows remain, but a beautiful city has been created. Margaret Coleman has lived in the area since 1968. A native of the West Coast, she was amazed at the history around Germantown and wrote this book to record the past and honor the planners of Germantown today. (Author's collection.)

Contents

Acknowledgments

This book would not have been possible without the remarkable memory of Jean King Phillips paired with her generosity in sharing her photographic collection, the history of her family and hometown, and the transcript of the Adzerodt trial. Thank you, Jean. Thank you, too, for reading the manuscript.

Margaret Leaman was extremely helpful. Thank you, Margaret. Many thanks to Valentina Sopko, Richard Katon, Vicki Crawford, Barbara McGraw, Garner W. Duvall, Arthur Virts, Susan Butler, Mike Knapp, the late Marian and Charles Jacobs, the late Eleanor Maughlin Young, the late Ella Virginia Gochenour, and the Montgomery County Historical Society for lending photographs and granting interviews. Sue Edwards, Germantown planner with Maryland-National Capital Park and Planning Commission, lent encouragement and read the manuscript. Thank you, Sue. Many photographs first appeared in *Montgomery County: A Pictorial History* by Margaret Coleman with photographer Anne Dennis Lewis. Thank you, Anne. Thank you, Lauren Bobier, editor. Research sources included a document titled, "War Department Washington D.C. April 26, 1865," the author's files, online informational sites, the Germantown Public Library, and the following:

Germantown: A Local History, Seneca Valley High School Honors English class of 1984;

Gaithersburg: The Heart of Montgomery County, William Hutchinson, et al., 1978;

A History of Germantown, Maryland, Susan Soderberg; 1988;

Montgomery County: A Pictorial History, Coleman and Lewis, 1983 and 1990;

Maryland-National Capital Park and Planning Commission publications, *Germantown Forward: Updating the Germantown Master Plan (1989)*, *Zoning and Highway Plan*; *Comprehensive Amendment to the Master Plan for Germantown Montgomery County, Maryland, 1974*; *Germantown Master Plan Information Open House, 2006*; *Community-wide Charrette, 2007*.

Unless otherwise noted, all images are from the author's collection.

Introduction

Every day is Christmas in Germantown, Maryland. Springing like Germelshausen from a small, rural village 20 years ago, Germantown today, were it incorporated, would be the second largest city in Maryland with a 2003 population of 85,000 and a 2008 estimate of 90,000.

Germantown is an exciting place to be. There is a multimillion-dollar library, a multimillion-dollar art center, a multimillion-dollar government center, and, on the outer cusp of the northern boundary, a multimillion-dollar jail. There is a regional shopping center and several smaller shopping areas. In the Town Center, wide streets are lined with pretty flowers, lovely street trees, affordable housing, and elegant townhouses. Most commercial buildings have matching facades, lending an aura of pleasing accord.

All the schools but one school are new. There are 12 elementary schools, 4 middle schools, 2 high schools, one special school, and a two-year college. Germantown has small shops, big-box stores, fine grocery stores, a police station, a fire station with a second one nearing completion, a tourist bureau, a 3,000-acre regional park, regional soccer fields and an aquatic center, senior housing, and two medical centers. County maintenance crews are seen constantly, keeping Germantown squeaky clean.

Newness fills the air, and each morning brings a new shop, new neighbors, a new school, a new set of townhouses.

In 1974, Germantown was a farming community of 2,000 in a county where growth is a Ping-Pong ball, bounced from one politician to the next. It's up, it's down, it's good, it's bad, it's out, it's in, but growth is always there, an established game in the county next door to the nation's capital.

Seeds of the new Germantown were sown in 1964 when the Maryland-National Capital Park and Planning Commission (M-NCPPC) adopted the General Plan for Orderly Development in the Maryland suburbs of Washington, D.C. The plan, called "On Wedges and Corridors," featured corridor cities radiating outward from the capital along major highways. Wedges of lower density lay within the corridors, preserving agriculture and open space.

Major development would adhere to the corridors and not sprawl into the wedges. Employment centers would cluster on either side of the highways. Shopping facilities and high-density housing would be built near this nucleus, and development would lessen to low density at the edge of the cities.

As I-270 and the headquarters of the Atomic Energy Commission were already in place, Germantown, Planning Area 19, was the natural choice for the first Montgomery County planned city. Looking toward Columbia, Maryland, and Reston, Virginia, a single contractor would construct everything, thus ensuring sympathetic correlation and an ongoing interest in the new city's success. Not all these dreams came true.

For 10 years, the professional planners at M-NCPPC studied the area, sketched plans, worked hard, and finally presented a comprehensive master plan for the orderly development of Germantown.

On the drawing board, Germantown morphed into six villages. The concept included Churchill Village, Neelsville Village, Middlebrook Village, Gunners Lake Village, Clopper Village, and Kingsview

Village. Surrounding the entire planning area would be a greenbelt of trees and parks. There were to be small parks in each village connected by bikeways and walkways, and each village would have at least one store. Rapid transit would be extended. Every inch of the 11,000-acre area was meticulously planned.

In 1974, the Germantown Master Plan was approved by M-NCPPC and the Montgomery County Executive and Council.

Germantown did not turn out exactly as planned, although the Montgomery County government held to the master plan as closely as conditions would permit.

Certain realities modified the vision, and situations arose that were beyond the control of M-NCPPC. The local rapid transit system was not extended. No single builder came forth. The fragmented land ownership in Planning Area 19 discouraged development by a single builder, and contracts for separate parcels of land were let to a variety of firms. The energy crisis affected sales, and prospective buyers worried as they watched President Carter wearing a sweater in the White House in spite of the solar panels he had installed on the roof. Furthermore, in the late 1970s to early 1980s, interest rates and housing prices soared out of reach of many buyers, and builders, worried about bankruptcy, jumped in and out of projects as quickly as they could. As townhouses were the cheapest to build and fastest to sell, more townhouses were built than the planners had specified.

But Germantown has always accepted change. Before 1974, Germantown had already moved twice. The 1865 Martinet and Bond map of Montgomery County shows Germantown as a small settlement at the intersection of Clopper and the Neelsville-Darnestown Roads, surrounded by the larger towns of Neelsville, Middlebrook, Boyd's Station, Darnestown, and Gaithersburg.

In 1873, the Metropolitan Branch of the Baltimore and Ohio Railroad swept through the county but missed Germantown. Residents picked up and moved, this time about a mile east to be nearer to the marvelous new method of transportation.

In 1954, an even faster public transport arrived, I-270. Germantown moved again and began to expand. M-NCPPC stepped in and managed the growth. And despite early growing pains, the professionally planned city is a thrill to behold. There are many areas of exquisite loveliness, and Germantown has a history of its own.

In the late 1700s, the English Waters family moved to the area now called Neelsville Village. Connecting the various Waterses was Waters Road, beginning at the National Road (Route 355) and ending at the former Route 118, now Liberty Mill Road.

Basil Waters and his wife, Anne Magruder Waters (daughter of Revolutionary War hero Col. Zadok Magruder), built a two-story brick home and named their place Pleasant Fields. In 1817, William Waters built a brick house elsewhere on Waters Road and painted it white. The descendants of both families settled along Waters Road. If the settlement ever had an English name, however, it is lost.

In the 1840s, German farmers settled near the intersection of two roads, Clopper and Germantown (now Liberty Mill) Roads. Some were from Pennsylvania, others from Germany. According to Jean King Phillips, whose family has been in Germantown since the 18th century, the English farmers already in the area began referring to the settlement as "where the Germans live." In time, the name became Germantown. Another source claims the Germans built shops. Needing a place name for the delivery of supplies, they ordered goods be delivered to Germantown.

Today one original German family remains in old Germantown, the John Upton Leaman family, descendants of the early Germans.

Germantown welcomes new residents, new business, new transportation methods, and new schools. Where every day is Christmas, life is good.

CHAPTER 1

HOMES AND GARDENS

Pleasant Fields, perhaps the oldest house in Germantown, was built around 1790 by Basil Waters, who inherited the 831 acres in 1788. Owned by the Waters family until 1933, Pleasant Fields fell victim to the Great Depression. In the early 1980s, the house, barns, and graveyard were purchased and restored by Montgomery County.

William and Maria Waters, the last children of Pleasant Fields, would be surprised to see the houses of Milestone on their pastureland. William is enjoying fishing in their farm pond. Maria looks like a French doll in her black gloves, high-buttoned boots, leg o'mutton sleeves, and small straw bowler. Today Pleasant Fields is the upcounty branch of the Montgomery County Historical Society (pictured above), and the pond site rests beside a hiker/biker trail in Milestone. (Vintage photograph courtesy of the late Charles and Marian Waters Jacobs.)

This Waters house was built in 1817 on land chartered to the William Waters family by Lord Baltimore. Numerous outbuildings and barns made the farm into a small village. Julian and Eleanor Cissel Waters were the last owners. During the Depression, Eleanor saved the farm for her family by selling farm produce at the Farm Womens Market in Bethesda. The Waters House apartment building was built on the same site. (Vintage photograph courtesy of Ella Virginia Waters Gochenour.)

Ballincara (pictured above), built by Joseph Leaman in the early 1800s, became the home of Andrew Baker from 1883 to 1930. Baker came back from the Klondike gold rush with a pocketful of money and spent it on Germantown. He made the house into a showplace with a swimming pool and gardens. The next owner turned Ballincara into the Marylander Home of Rest in 1949. The house was burned by the fire department in 1980. Today the site is the Landmark Townhouses. (Vintage photograph courtesy of the Montgomery County Historical Society [MCHS].)

The Grusendorf/Dunn Log House (pictured below in 1972), built by Germans who settled the area around Clopper and Germantown Roads around 1841, became part of a larger house that burned in 1982. Located on the east side of Clopper between Liberty Mill and Route 119, the cabin was moved to Seneca Creek State Park and partially restored. Today it watches over the ruins of Woodland, the elegant former home of Francis Clopper. (Vintage photograph courtesy of Margaret Leaman.)

The Charles Bowman family (pictured below) poses in front of their new home near Cedar Grove. Founders of Germantown's chief industry, Bowman Brothers Mill, shipped their Silver Leaf Flour around the world. At the second largest mill in Maryland, livestock feed and cornmeal were also available. Today a rusted bicycle and lawn mower mark the approximate place where the house once stood. Today's Germantown leader is county council chairman Mike Knapp, shown above with his family. (Vintage photograph courtesy of Jean King Phillips; modern photograph courtesy of Mike Knapp.)

Londonderry (pictured above) was the dowry gift to Joseph Neel's daughter, Rosanna, when she married Rev. J. H. S. Henderson in 1862. In 1927, the house was moved across the road to the site of today's Milestone Giant. Then it became a convent for elderly nuns followed by a group home featuring unusual parties. Philip Milestone bought the property in 1990 and sold it to Aris Mardissian, who sold the house for $10 to be moved 1.5 miles. Today Londonderry is a private home. (Vintage photograph courtesy of MCHS.)

The Hanshew house (pictured above) stood in the middle of today's Crystal Rock Drive. It is significant for the sociology it demonstrates. Depicted is a comfortable late-Victorian lifestyle with a 12-member family in front of a large house with pretty gardens. Separate from the family group is a black woman holding the baby. Today the wide street and attractive commercial building announce the big changes of new Germantown. (Vintage photograph courtesy of MCHS.)

This farmhouse (pictured below) once focused national attention on Germantown. Fame came with George Adzerodt, coconspirator of John Wilkes Booth in the Lincoln assassination plot. Here Adzerodt grew up, and here he was captured. Adzerodt's cousin, Hartman Richter, was the owner at the time. In 1933, Herbert King bought the farm from Richter heirs. The house burned in 1982, and new housing claims the site. (Vintage photograph courtesy of Jean King Phillips.)

Mature trees mark the former site of the Hargett house (pictured below), built by John Hargett. His children—Anna, Margaret, Wesley, and Harold—became prominent residents of Germantown and Boyds. Wesley worked as a heating system specialist, and Harold bought a farm near Boyds. During World War II, Germans returned to Germantown as prisoners of war and filled a need on farms, including Hargett's. Cherished as good workers, the prisoners became their captors' friends, exchanging visits after the war. (Vintage photograph courtesy of MCHS.)

Hanson and Martha Anne Ricketts emigrated from Ireland and built this farmhouse on Darnestown Road (pictured above). Bessie Hommiller stands beside them. Bessie probably arrived on an orphan train. Between 1854 and 1929, about 200,000 orphaned or abandoned children were sent by train from New York to find someone to care for them. Bessie was lucky; she found a good home. The site is now the Jewish Center of North Potomac. (Vintage photograph courtesy of Elsie Curliss Boyer.)

The Home Place was built by Christian Leaman in 1867. German families included Leaman, Grussendorf, Dunn, Snyder, and Rhinehart, who intermarried and were major contributors to the community. John Upton Leaman was born in this house. Today the house is handsomely restored in the Carlson Farm neighborhood on Riffle Ford Road. (Vintage photograph courtesy of Margaret Leaman.)

This handsome house with the fish scale–shingled gable and unusual roof was located on Germantown (now Boland Farm) Road and Route 240 (now Route 355). Four generations of the Dr. William H. Benson family owned the approximately 200-acre farm. There were beautiful gardens, a goldfish pond, terra-cotta pillars with ferns, and rolling lawns. Today the site is the Free State gas station. (Vintage photograph courtesy of MCHS.)

Gracious living of the Gay Nineties was enjoyed by Col. James Boyd at his home, Bonnie Brae. In this picture, the old gentleman is cared for by a nurse as his wife, Sara, relaxes under a shady tree and is waited on by two women. A windmill provided running water in the house. Today only the stone entrance pillars remain. Most of Boyd's farm is underwater, and the remainder is owned by Montgomery County. (Vintage photograph courtesy of the late Eleanor Maughlin Young.)

In 1866, James Boyd built this house (pictured above) for David Maughlin, his nephew and farm manager. The Maughlin farm was purchased for Little Seneca Lake and is partly underwater, but the house was built on higher ground and remains. Now the house is protected by the county's master plan and Ordinance for Historic Preservation and is the home of John and Christine DeReggi. (Vintage photograph courtesy of Eleanor Maughlin Young.)

In the splendid days when railroad was king and Boyds was its crown jewel, Winderbourne was built in the best Great Gatsby tradition. Mary Howe Totten rode an excursion train and was enchanted with the prettiest spot on the Metropolitan Branch, the James Boyd farm (pictured above). She built a home and named it for the winder (bobbin) invented by her uncle, Elias Howe. Today Little Seneca Lake encircles Winderbourne on three sides.

The railroad was delighted with the scene Winderbourne provided and paid half the cost of a bridge over the tracks, giving Winderbourne access to Clopper Road (pictured below). In the best Victorian tradition, Winderbourne was painted pale pink with darker pink trim and deep-rose-colored shutters. The railroad wrapped around Winderbourne on three sides like a toy train, preceding the path of Lake Seneca. Shown is the approximate location of the Winderbourne bridge today. (Vintage photograph courtesy of Hershey Ayton.)

In 1768, Thomas Drury built this log cabin (pictured below) in the wilderness. Jonathan Austin bought it in 1804 and built the frame section. Abandoned in 1951, the house began to slip back into the ground. The author and her husband purchased the cabin and restored it with help from friends and professionals. Now listed on the National Register of Historic Places, the house is joyful and useful again.

This Clarksburg house (pictured above) delightfully retains its history. Built in 1911 as a 12-room home, through the years, the house served as a fabric store, a bridal shop, and an antiques emporium. Today "The Bustle is Back," according to owners Newland Communities. Handsomely restored, the house declares the proud history of Clarksburg and proclaims its prosperous future.

In 1922, gardens produced food. In today's Germantown, gardens offer beauty. Beneath the above picture, an extension agent wrote, "No need to fear the food administration with a farm garden like this." Now Joe Simone ("Boca Joe") creates a tropical paradise at his Germantown townhouse with oleander, palms, deep scarlet mandevilla, hibiscus, elephant ears, bananas, and more. (Vintage photograph courtesy of the Montgomery County Extension Office.)

CHAPTER 2

FARMS

In 1950, George and Shirley Butler purchased a 37-acre farm with a log home and poultry house and began to plant. Today their children and grandchildren live on the farm, caring for over 300 acres filled with peaches, apples, blueberries, raspberries, strawberries, flowers, Christmas trees, and pumpkins. Shown is Butler's Orchard in 1951. (Photograph courtesy of Susan Butler.)

Phillips Farm set up a stand at the Shaker Festival in 2000. Now Jean King Phillips stands in the doorway of her current farm market on the last 13 acres of her father's farm to remain in family hands (pictured above). A petting zoo with farm animals and a corn maze attract the families of Germantown to buy fresh, local produce and meet the creatures that yesterday's Germantown children knew so well. (Vintage photograph courtesy of Jean King Phillips.)

Five generations of one family farmed Kingsbury's Orchards. In 1907, Edwin Horine purchased the land. His son John Horine loved a ripe peach. John planted the orchard now managed by Peggy Horine Kingsbury and her son, Gene Kingsbury. A customer painted the stand in the 1930s. Today Peggy holds the Kingsbury Peach (pictured below), a new cultivar developed by Gene. In 2006, Kingsbury's Orchards was given the Royce Hanson Award for agricultural preservation. (Vintage photograph courtesy of Peggy Horine Kingsbury.)

Herbert King once owned all the land between Schaeffer and Germantown Roads from Clopper Road to the Soccerplex and farmed 1,000 acres. Behind the small girl on the pony, King's fields of corn appear endless, marching into the horizon beyond. Today a new Montgomery County Fire Department station is under construction at Germantown and Clopper Roads, marking the opposite end of the King farm. (Vintage photograph courtesy of Jean King Phillips.)

In 1811, Lott Linthicum bought land called Panther's Ridge and established this farm on Old Baltimore Road (pictured below). Lott's grandson Charles Linthicum built the current house in 1927. Ayrshire cattle grazed beside Little Seneca Creek in 1970. Today houses sprout on Linthicum's fertile fields, and Observation Drive will soon be extended through the dairy barn. The 2008 picture is taken from the top of the ridge near the barns, looking down at the stream valley.

This is the meticulously maintained bank barn (pictured below) of Hunter, Donald, and Earl Staley. Bank barns had two levels and generally were built on slopes, with the larger upper section at ground level to accommodate vehicles and store hay for winter feeding. The lower level was for livestock. Staley's dairy farm is now Henley Hall, a community of 21 lots with small farms, equestrian trails, sweeping green pastures, and views of Sugarloaf Mountain. Valentina Sopko grooms her horse, Julius, at her Henley Hall home, Four Winds Farm.

Macie Schaeffer King stands beside her 1926 farmhouse (pictured above). The founding president of the Farm Womens Cooperative Market in Bethesda was an important community leader, as was her husband, James, the second president of the prestigious county farm bureau. Their farm is now the South Germantown Recreational Park and Maryland Soccerplex. The house is gone but the barn remains, owned by the King Barn Dairy MOOseum. (Vintage photograph courtesy of Garner W. Duvall and Barbara McGraw.)

John Upton Leaman (pictured above) uses a spring-toothed harrow on the land of his ancestral farm established by the family of his mother, Augusta Grussendorf Leaman. Belle and Queenie provide reusable energy. Today the last farm on Clopper Road is being developed into apartment houses, town houses, and single-family homes. The Leaman farmhouse remains, an honored relic of the Germans who settled Germantown. (Vintage photograph courtesy of the late Idella Leaman and Margaret Leaman.)

Recalling Germantown's past, this bank barn (pictured below) stood on Germantown Road opposite Riffle Ford Road. A slope was created on the upper level of bank barns for vehicular entrance into an area for threshing wheat and storing hay. Below, animals had access to shelter. Green hay could cause combustion, hence the many windows. Today there are few cows but 12,000 horses in Montgomery County. Shown is an elegant new equestrian barn near Germantown. (Vintage photograph courtesy of Jean King Phillips.)

Walter Johnson (pictured below, fourth from right), "The Big Train," was a baseball great of the Washington Senators and Cleveland Indians and a Maryland state delegate. Johnson loved to foxhunt. He opened wide the windows of his farmhouse across from today's Germantown Post Office to hear the foxhounds sing. Today foxhunting is enjoyed by members of the Potomac Hunt in Boyds. (Vintage photograph courtesy of the late Malcomb Walter; modern photograph courtesy of Vicki Crawford.)

CHAPTER 3

Business and Industry

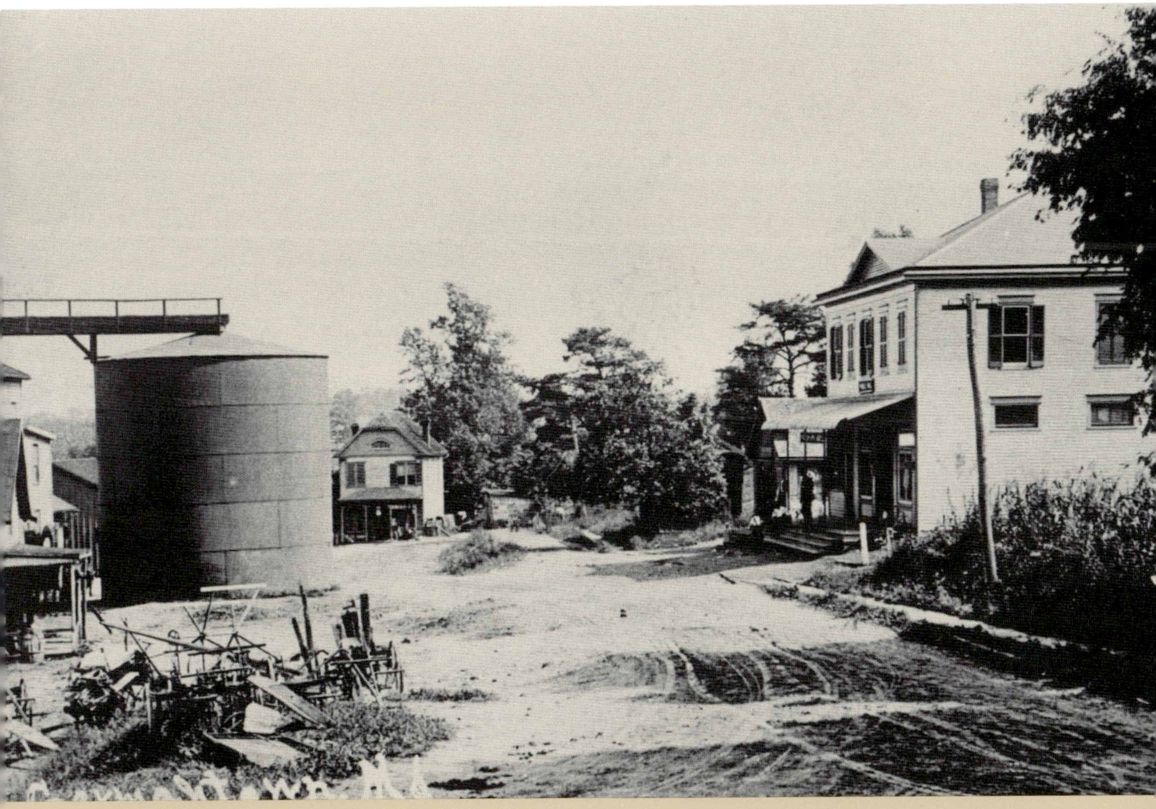

Germantown shopped here. Everything from lengths of cloth to a medium-rare steak could be purchased at the general store and post office on the right. Opposite the store were the mill and various small industries. The store was originally owned by Perry and Richard Waters; the last owner was Herbert King. (Vintage photograph courtesy of the late Idella Leaman.)

Industry exploded in Germantown with the 1888 advent of Bowman Brothers Mill (pictured above). Introduced by the train, steam energy was fast and reliable, and the old water-powered mills were instantly outmoded. Bountiful crops of grains flourished in the fields around Germantown and were milled into feed, flour, and cornmeal. A commercial building of today occupies a site in the corporate center. (Vintage photograph courtesy of Jean King Phillips.)

The original mill burned and was rebuilt about 1914 by the Bowman brothers. In 1918, Liberty Milling Company bought the mill and continued the business, recording annual sales up to $1 million. Reflecting the soaring heights is the Qiagen building on Germantown Road. Instead of grinding grains, Qiagen makes tools researchers need to extract and purify nucleic acids in DNA/RNA and provides DNA sequencing services. (Vintage photograph courtesy of Jean King Phillips.)

An essential implement for the mill's success was this scale house (pictured below). Horse-drawn wagons, then trucks, pulled on to the platform. Their loads were weighed, their wheat or corn unloaded, and their vehicle re-weighed to determine payment. Flour and livestock feed were bagged inside the mill and available in 5- to 100-pound sacks. The rusty scale is still there, although the tiny building is overgrown with trees and brush and partially hidden from view. (Vintage photograph courtesy of Jean King Phillips.)

Black Rock Mill (left), built in 1815, ground grain into flour and also sawed wood into building material. Seneca Creek rushes wide and clear beside the mill. Traces of the dam and millpond may still be seen. When steam replaced water as a more powerful energy source, Black Rock milled lumber to build Bowman Brothers Mill. Now owned by the National Park Service, the mill has been partially restored, testifying to the early history of the mill era. (Vintage photograph courtesy of the late Idella Leaman.)

A whisper away from busy Clopper Road loom the ruins of Clopper Mill (pictured below), built in 1834. Seneca Creek provided energy to mill wheat into flour and corn into meal. Francis Cassatt Clopper added a woolen mill, making blankets for Civil War soldiers. Today the mill is part of Seneca Creek State Park. Its empty windows wink at the cars through leafy lashes, nearly hidden by sycamores and brush. (Vintage photograph courtesy of the late Idella Leaman.)

Adventure awaits on Germantown's outskirts! An entrancing ruin, 150 feet long (pictured above), fronts a seam of red sandstone at Tschiffley Mill near Seneca. Stone was cut and shipped to Washington via canal to build the Smithsonian Institute's castle. Locally houses, barns, walls, and fences were constructed of Seneca sandstone. Descendants of Jack Clipper, (below) second from right, remain in the area. Today the site is part of the Chesapeake and Ohio Canal National Park. (Vintage photograph courtesy of Bernice Clipper.)

Charles T. Johnson lived with his wife and children in this house, pictured in about 1895. Johnson was the postmaster, a very important job. Later Carlton Browning was the rural route carrier, and his house is shown. Browning is remembered for his kindly service and for the valentine he delivered to each home on his route. The valentine was a photograph taken in 1910 of a man in a horse-drawn cart handing a letter to a pretty young lady and, with the letter, a kiss. (Courtesy of the late Idella Leaman.)

Margaret Leaman, a lifelong resident of Germantown, began working in the tiny post office in the general store in 1928 and was postmaster from 1943 to 1971. In 1969, the new Germantown Post Office opened across from the school that can be glimpsed through her window. In 1991, a newer post office opened. Germantown postmaster Lakhuit K. Dheman sits in a comfortable chair and sorts mail by computer. (Vintage photograph courtesy of Margaret Leaman.)

Edith "Miss Edie" Austin (right) was the postmaster of Boyds from the late 1940s to 1965. She lived in a log cabin with no electricity or plumbing, heated by a fireplace. She carried her lunch and water to work and used a privy across the road. She wore homemade dresses, black cotton stockings, and blue tennis shoes. Today's postmaster, Glorious "Glo" Cooper (below), sorts mail mostly by computer. Part of Germantown has a Boyds zip code, melding the communities. (Vintage photograph courtesy of Arthur G. Virts Jr.)

Look what someone could do at the Clarksburg Post Office (below)—tie up a horse, buy gas, and use a telephone. For 200 years, Clarksburg thrived and Germantown crept. Today Clarksburg is Germantown's younger sister, designed by professional planners at M-NCPPC, who declare Clarksburg is the county's last planned city. From a population of 1891 in 2000, Clarksburg's estimate in 2008 is 6,000. (Vintage photograph courtesy of the late Clarence Day.)

Horace Waters's store (pictured below) stood in old Germantown at the intersection of Clopper and Germantown (now Liberty Mill) Roads. Waters wrote purchases in a ledger and collected monthly. No one paid cash. Shortly after this picture was taken, Waters was killed by a robber who found no more than a few cents. Today's Town Center is alive with many restaurants and shops, the art center, the library, and a government facility. (Vintage photograph courtesy of Jean King Phillips; modern photograph courtesy of Sue Edwards, M-NCPPC.)

In 1925, Andrew Baker came home from visiting Florida enchanted with roadside fruit stands built in the shape of huge oranges. One of Maryland's busiest roads bordered his property, and Baker's orchards were producing copious amounts of apples—a perfect equation for business. The Volstead Act, 1919–1933, made hard cider illegal but delicious fresh cider was perfectly legal. Now owned by the county, the landmark awaits a new use. (Vintage photograph courtesy of Jean King Phillips.)

In 1929, Andrew Baker's heirs sold the Cider Barrel to the Cross family, who installed a restaurant, tourist cottages, and mobile home court (pictured above), as well as continuing the cider business. Trailer owners were delighted to find such a beautiful wooded site and parked carefully beneath the tall trees. Bill Cross sold the land in 2002 and poured the last glass of cider that same fall. Today the site is filled with the 316 apartments of the Elms (pictured below). (Vintage photograph courtesy of MCHS.)

Germantown's first car agency featured the Buick automobile (pictured below), made in the USA. Located on the west side of the Germantown Presbyterian Chapel was Jacob Snyder's blacksmith shop–cum–automobile repair and showplace; the site is currently empty. Jacob Snyder's family was among the first to arrive from Germany. Today German-made luxury cars grace the Mercedes-Benz agency in the Town Center. (Vintage photograph courtesy of Jean King Phillips.)

Construction begins on the 1982 addition at the Germantown Medical Center, Germantown Road, Route 118. Richard Katon, M.D., built a 35,000-square-foot clinic attached to the historic house (pictured below) in an example of historic preservation handsomely done. Today a medical laboratory is housed here, and doctors' offices and medical facilities occupy the two floors. A commodious parking lot is located behind the clinic. (Vintage photograph courtesy of Dr. Richard Katon.)

When Dr. Katon looked out his window in 1982, he had a view of cows, pasture, Route 355, and a few distant buildings foretelling the birth of new Germantown (pictured above). Germantown Meats stood between the cattle and Germantown Road. Today the pasture is Observation Drive and houses. Germantown Meats is long gone, and the road in front of Germantown Medical Center has been renamed Boland Farm. (Vintage photograph courtesy of Dr. Richard Katon.)

Until recent years, Germantown book lovers went to the library in Gaithersburg or patronized the weekly bookmobile. In the year 2000, the Upcounty Regional Services Center opened and the largest first-floor space became the library. In 2007, the Germantown Public Library (pictured below) opened at a cost of $19 million. Now library space is enlarged from 16,000 to 44,193 square feet on two levels. There are 180,000 volumes on the shelves, and 37 PCs available for public use.

In the glory days of Boyds, there were two gas stations, an Esso and a Gulf (pictured below). The High Store, far right, had many steps, but it was the second story that caused a rumpus. James Boyd built it with a large space upstairs for meetings and dances. Boyd came from Scotland in 1844 and likely put on his kilts and danced the schottische. Today the empty arm of the Esso sign points to wires, unseen in 1936.

George Washington slept here (pictured below). In 1754, Michael Ashford Dowden built this ordinary, or inn. On their way to Fort Duquesne April 15–17, 1755, Gen. Edward Braddock and his young surveyor, George Washington, stayed here as the troops camped on the hillside. Andrew Jackson dined here in 1829. Located in Clarksburg, the site is currently empty. Wouldn't Michael Ashford Dowden be surprised to see the view outside his window? (Vintage photograph courtesy of the late Mr. and Mrs. Clarence Day.)

A trading post on the Old Sinnaca Indian Trail attracted John Clark to build his home and store on the site in 1780 (pictured above). Clarksburg became an important 19th-century town with a distillery, tanner, bone mill (for fertilizer), and its own town band. When the train skipped Clarksburg, the town declined. For years, the building was abandoned, but today the town is revitalized. An organic market is open in the historic structure.

On November 7, 1944, residents of Barnesville put on their suits, ties, and white shirts and went to vote in their town hail, electing Franklin Delano Roosevelt and Harry Truman. Only one woman is in line (pictured above), wearing shiny rayon stockings with her good dark suit, white shirt, and little hat. Today Barnesville votes at Monocacy schoolhouse and no one wears a suit and tie. Now the polls, like the post office, are run with computers. (Vintage photograph courtesy of the Library of Congress.)

CHAPTER 4

Schools, Churches, and the Civil War

All the Germantown eighth graders in 1926 are shown in this picture: seven girls and three boys. Among them is Eleanor Ardella Louise Bowman (King), Germantown School class of 1929. Today's Germantown sixth through eighth graders go to middle schools Martin Luther King Jr. (857 students), Kingsview (938 students), Neelsville (727 students), or Roberto W. Clemente (1,132 students). (Vintage photograph courtesy of Jean King Phillips.)

In this photograph (below) of Neelsville Public School are scions of most east Germantown families in May 1904. Included are members of the Waters, Dowden, Neel, Gardner, Burdette, Boyer, Harding, Linthicum, King (Lawson and Forest), Henderson, and Howes families. Listing them on the reverse side was Maria Waters of Pleasant Fields (second row, fourth from right). Today there are a lot more children in Neelsville. They may attend Dr. Sally K. Ride Elementary School with 545 students (above). (Vintage photograph courtesy of MCHS.)

Germantown's traditional four-square, two-story school topped the hill now flanked by Dawson Farm Road and Germantown Road, facing Liberty Mill Road. Maryland established public schools for white children in 1860 when the frills of education included plane trigonometry, surveying, chemistry, botany, elocution, manners and morals, Latin, and orthography. Shown (left) is the fifth-grade class at the old school and (below) Germantown Elementary today. (Vintage photograph courtesy of Ella Virginia Waters Gochenour.)

From 1910 until 1934, Germantown's children climbed a steep hill to school. At recess, they flocked to the playground (pictured above) at street level in front of the school. Properly dressed schoolgirls played gentle games, and a tall hedge kept them safe. In 1934, the current school was built at the lower level and the playground moved to the former school site. The school today is one of 12 elementary schools in Germantown. (Vintage photograph courtesy of Jean King Phillips.)

Germantown Colored School, which existed about 1885–1910, was the former white school of 1860 (pictured below). Desegregation was an agonizing affair, and after 1954, good people of both colors worked hard to overcome the past. Shown above is Spark M. Matsunaga Elementary School and Longview School, where 1,152 students of all races gather daily both inside the building and in one of the triple row of temporary classrooms outside. (Vintage photograph courtesy of Jean King Phillips.)

Boyd Negro School, 1895–1936, was an abandoned building in 1979 (pictured below). The Boyds/Clarksburg/Germantown Historical Society was founded and the schoolhouse saved. Restored with public funds and sweat equity from members, the schoolhouse welcomed returning students in 1982 to celebrate the restoration. Their former teacher, Lillian Giles, is pictured above, in the first row, second from left. Today Clarksburg and Germantown have separate historical societies, and the Boyds organization is led by Elaine Fors-Davis.

The Arabian Horse Museum, built in 1966, honored the Arabian breed of pleasure horses (pictured above). Founded by Ruth McCormick Tankersley, the museum held a wide assortment of artifacts, including a life-sized statue of Indraff, Tankersley's silver stallion. Arabian arches were retained throughout expansion, lending enchantment. Today Barnesville School is a private, country day school located in the county's agricultural preserve and serving pre-kindergarten through the eighth grade. (Tile courtesy of Anne Tankersley Sturm.)

The children of Chesapeake and Ohio Canal and Tschiffley Mill workers needed a schoolhouse, and the plentiful red Seneca sandstone of River Road made the ideal building material. Now restored and administered by Historic Medley District, Inc., the schoolhouse welcomes classes from Germantown and elsewhere to time travel with their program, a Typical Day in 1880, at the Seneca Sandstone Schoolhouse (pictured below). (Vintage photograph courtesy of Historic Medley District, Inc.)

Until 1974, Germantown's closest high school was in Gaithersburg. From 1905 to 1950, this traditional two-story building on North Summit Avenue (pictured below) held students in grades 1–11. In 1936, the school graduated 24 teens from the first four-year high school program. A new high school was completed in 1951 for 800 students in grades 7–12. In 1974, Seneca Valley High School opened; it holds 1,687 students today. Northwest High opened in 1998 with 2,000 students today. (Vintage photograph courtesy of the late Idella Leaman.)

Montgomery College, Germantown Campus, opened October 21, 1978, with two buildings, 1,200 students, and a faculty of 24. A steel water tower modeled Planet Earth as seen from a satellite. By 2003, enrollment was 5,000 with 80 faculty members in four buildings. A 40-acre biotechnology laboratory is nearing completion in 2008. (Vintage photograph courtesy of Anne Dennis Lewis.)

Neelsville Presbyterian Church once anchored the eastern end of Germantown Road. The log Darnestown Presbyterian Church stood at the western end and Germantown Presbyterian Chapel in the middle. The Neelsville church built an addition and then a much larger one but fortuitously retained the historic chapel, which is now used by small congregations and for weddings and special occasions (pictured below). (Vintage photograph courtesy of the late Idella Leaman.)

A quiet dirt road once connected Neelsville with Darnestown Presbyterian Churches and was called Germantown Road. When Germantown moved a mile east to be near the railroad, Presbyterians built this chapel (right). The building became a veterinary clinic and now has multiple uses. Germantown Road relocated, and this road is now called Walter Johnson Road. (Vintage photograph courtesy of the late Idella Leaman.)

Church is the place where emotions are nurtured and controversy may arise. Such was the case with Germantown Methodists at the time of the War Between the States. Strong feelings flared like rockets over Richmond, and the Methodist Church broke in two. Shown below is the Methodist Church South. The restored building with new windows, sans bell tower and vestibule (shown above), is now the Family Medical Center, and the Methodists are together again. (Vintage photograph courtesy of the late Idella Leaman.)

Looking very much as it did when Francis Clopper built it around 1834 is historic St. Rose of Lima Chapel. During the Civil War, a Confederate soldier died nearby, and Clopper buried him secretly at night to avoid prosecution for aiding the enemy. Later Fr. John Cuddy pastored here until his untimely death by a train. Today a large new sanctuary holds services, and the chapel hosts small ceremonies. (Vintage photograph courtesy of MCHS.)

George Adzerodt (left) grew up in Germantown, left home, and found himself in Washington, D.C. He took a room in the home of Mary Surratt and met her son John and his friend John Wilkes Booth. Adzerodt accepted the task of assassinating Vice President Johnson. He couldn't do it and returned to his childhood home. Along the way, he had Easter dinner with Hezekiah Metz, whose home was approximately at South Gunners Branch Park. (Vintage photograph courtesy of the Library of Congress.)

At 2:00 p.m., April 19, 1865, U.S. Army intelligence officer James Purdum got an urgent message from Nathan Page: George Adzerodt was a few miles away in Germantown. There was a $25,000 reward for his capture. Purdum collected troops and arrested Adzerodt, his cousin Hartman Richter, and the Metz dinner guests. Adzerodt was hanged on July 7, 1865, with Mary Surratt, Lewis Paine, and Davy Herold. Shown is Purdum's home, now destroyed. Next door to the site is Black Hills' Butterfly Garden.

CHAPTER 5

TRANSPORTATION

Train wrecks are rare, but when they do happen, they cause havoc. About 3:00 a.m. on a late fall night in 1986, James "Bud" and Rachie Gwynn were sleeping in their upstairs bedroom. As was their habit, they never heard the train. Suddenly a coupling broke; the train derailed and sliced the house neatly in two. Bud and Rachie stepped out of their bedroom onto the engine and slid to the ground. No one was injured. The engineer took a job at the post office.

Designed by E. Francis Baldwin, chief architect for the Baltimore and Ohio Railroad, this elegant brick station (pictured below) with slate roof and iron roof crest was named Boyd's Station. In 1928, engineers widening the track attempted to move the station but were unsuccessful. A smaller station was built, but it, too, is gone, and a Plexiglas shelter now keeps the rain off waiting passengers. (Vintage photograph courtesy of the late Nell Staley.)

In 1928, the railroad track was doubled and straightened between Germantown and Boyds. Arthur Virts Sr. walks the track, ready to pull the lever near his left arm (pictured above). This motion will move the track, allowing passage to the double line. In the background, grain is loaded from the Gambril and Carlin Mill into a boxcar on a siding. Telegraph poles connect the world with this important town. Today the only historic structure remaining is Hoyles Mill, used for storage. (Vintage photograph courtesy of Arthur G. Virts Jr.)

Before the overpass was built in Boyds, crossing arms kept people and vehicles off the track when a train was coming. The arms and lights worked by batteries, and the station and tracks were on a level plane with the town (pictured above). Today there is no signal at Boyds because the train is elevated, but at Germantown (below), lights flash and signals call to keep pedestrians off the tracks when a train is near. (Vintage photograph courtesy of the late Nell Staley.)

In 1910, Boyds was a bustling town (pictured below). Up steep steps is the town hall meeting place, general store, and post office. On the right is Benjamin Hicks's store. A third general store belonged to Mahlon T. Lewis and James Williams. Two steam-powered mills provided industry, and summer boardinghouses were plentiful. There were three schools. Today Boyds is a pleasant community protected by the county's master plan of historic districts. New homes and small farms surround history. (Vintage photograph courtesy of Arthur G. Virts Jr.)

The wooden bridge over Seneca Creek (pictured below) was an engineering fable in 1873. Gandy dancers pounced on sparks after each crossing, and soldiers camped beneath it during World War I. Chief engineer James Boyd was highly respected. When he died on Christmas Eve 1896, all the trains on the Metropolitan Branch stopped at Boyd's Station. In 1928, the track was straightened and the bridge abandoned. Today the site is the dam for Little Seneca Lake. (Vintage photograph courtesy of the late Leroy Morgan.)

This is Henderson's Corner in 1929. Rev. J. H. S. Henderson was the minister at the Neelsville and Germantown Presbyterian churches from 1864–1882. Today the intersection bearing his name (pictured below) has been relocated and is linked with another pastor, Fr. Leonard F. Hurley, the Catholic priest who served Germantown from 1974 to 1987. Father (now Monsignor) Hurley established the Mother Seton parish and built the church on Father Hurley Boulevard. (Vintage photograph courtesy of MCHS.)

"Country road, take me home." When Bill Danoff and Taffy Nivert wrote the song John Denver made famous, they were driving on Clopper Road (pictured above). The year was 1971. Twice daily, traffic on Clopper Road halted as cows crossed from the Leaman Farm to their pasture. Russell Phillips restored an old Methodist cemetery for his Eagle Scout badge. Now a deeper, wider Clopper Road fills with cars, and the cemetery has no access. (Vintage photograph courtesy of Jean King Phillips.)

This historic road, Route 355 (pictured below), was created by Native Americans; sketched by Benjamin Latrobe in 1802; and trod upon by George Washington and Gen. Edward Braddock in the French and Indian War, Gen. Jubal Early in the Civil War, and Jacob Coxey's Army of the Unemployed in 1894. Photographed in Clarksburg at the general store and post office, the historic store is now restored and open for business. It features organic food. (Vintage photograph courtesy of Clarence Day.)

Germantown gets to Virginia in one of four ways—driving I-495, swimming, walking (in September), or taking the Gen. Jubal Early at White's Ferry, chartered in 1782. Purchased by Confederate colonel Elijah Veirs White after the war, the ferry was named for his commanding officer. Shown is the Esch family (pictured below) crossing the Potomac in their 1923 Mitchell and the Gen. Jubal Early today. Through the years, the boats have been replaced, but they all operated by cable on the starboard side. (Vintage photograph courtesy of Neal and Marian Esch Potter.)

CHAPTER 6

Ten Mile

Once a village lay beneath the waters of Little Seneca Lake, the watery divide between Germantown and Boyds. Ten Mile Creek flowed through a valley of wildflowers, farms, and an inn, as shown. In 1978, Montgomery County joined Washington Suburban Sanitary Commission to build a dam where the high railroad trestle had been and fill the valley with a 525-acre reservoir as an emergency water supply for Prince George's and Montgomery Counties. (Photograph courtesy of the late Nell Staley.)

Summer boarders rode the train to the Fleet Staley Hotel (pictured above), fleeing the heat and humidity of pre-air-conditioned Washington. Fleet's son Ralph met the trains and transported the boarders along Ten Mile Creek Road to the inn. On the creekside, Fleet installed a Beauty Spot with a swimming hole, swings, tables, and benches. Boarders drank sweet, fresh milk; ate fresh meats and vegetables; and played in the stream. A birdhouse marks the site of the Boyd farm. (Vintage photograph courtesy of the late Nell Staley.)

Georgia Rose Lawson lived in the big cement house (pictured below) her husband built to replace the tall Victorian that mysteriously burned down when they moved to Boyds. Wilfred Lawson taught at Tennessee State College and fulfilled a dream when he and Georgia bought the 162 acres in 1937. Wilfred was killed by his bull in 1943. The house can be seen near the upper left of the lake photograph.

This is the home (pictured below) purchased by Georgia and Wilfred Lawson—a Chautauqua house where literary lectures and musical performances were held. The house perched high above the beautiful valley. Within a short carriage ride was Boyd's Station, providing easy transportation to the city. Today a charming new house sits on the site and looks down at the lake. (Vintage photograph courtesy of the late Georgia Lawson.)

Georgia Lawson's chestnut barn (pictured above) housed Jersey cows. After Dr. Wilfred Lawson's death, Georgia stayed on the farm and hired farm managers, including Marilee Hershberger. Serving on national and local boards, often as chairperson, Lawson's wide range of friends included First Lady Eleanor Roosevelt. Lawson raised two granddaughters and a great-granddaughter here. A native of Haiti, she knew no differences of wealth, race, or position. Her son James said, "She sat where she liked on the bus."

Ten Mile Creek School served the children of Boyds from 1870 to school consolidation in 1936. Two of the students pictured above were wards of the orphan court of Baltimore. Walter Melvin (seated far right) came on the orphan train and never left Boyds. The schoolhouse was converted into a dwelling in 1942. (Vintage photograph courtesy of the late Walter Melvin.)

Ten Mile Creek flows timelessly through its doomed valley. Below is the new bridge under construction. Trees have been topped and left for the benefit of fish, and the old Boyd farm is seen at top right. On the center horizon is Germantown rising. At the right, a farm truck travels Ten Mile Creek Road. Today water is released in times of drought to supply Washington Suburban Sanitary Commission customers, and the lake and park provide recreation and serene beauty for Germantown and Boyds. (Vintage photograph courtesy of Charles McGovern.)